WITH LOVE
TO MY FRIEND

Hallmark Editions

Selected by Aileene Herrbach Neighbors.   Designed by Rainer K. Koenig.

The publisher wishes to thank those who have given their kind permission to reprint material included in this book. Every effort has been made to give proper acknowledgments. Any omissions or errors are deeply regretted, and the publisher, upon notification, will be pleased to make necessary corrections in subsequent editions.

ACKNOWLEDGMENTS: Excerpt by Kahlil Gibran from *A Third Treasury of Kahlil Gibran.* © 1975, 1973, 1966, 1965 by Philosophical Library, Inc. Reprinted by permission of The Citadel Press, Inc. Excerpt by Erich Fromm abridged from pp. 24 and 25 in *The Art of Loving* by Erich Fromm, Volume Nine in the World Perspective Series, edited by Ruth Nanda Anshen. Copyright © 1956 by Erich Fromm. Reprinted by permission of Harper & Row, Publishers, Inc. and George Allen & Unwin, Ltd. Excerpt from *Living by Faith* by Faith Baldwin. Copyright © 1962, 1963, 1964 by Faith Baldwin Cuthrell. Reprinted by permission of Holt, Rinehart and Winston, Publishers. "By Messenger" from *The Complete Poetical Works of Amy Lowell.* © 1955 by Houghton Mifflin Company. Reprinted by permission of the publisher. "The Net" reprinted with permission of Macmillan Publishing Co., Inc. from *Collected Poems* by Sara Teasdale. Copyright 1920 by Macmillan Publishing Co., Inc. Renewed 1948 by Mamie T. Wheless. "You are a mirror . . ." from *Aim for a Star* by Helen Lowrie Marshall. Copyright © 1964 by Helen Lowrie Marshall. Reprinted by arrangement. "You are you . . ." by Frederick S. Perls. © 1969 Real People Press. Reprinted by arrangement. "The first stage . . ." from "The Dogwood Tree: A Boyhood" by John Updike from *Five Boyhoods*, edited by Martin Levin. © 1962 by Martin Levin. Published by Doubleday and Company, Inc. Reprinted by permission of Martin Levin.

© 1977, Hallmark Cards, Inc., Kansas City, Missouri. Printed in the United States of America. Standard Book Number: 87529-527-4.

Today I have been happy...
I held the memory of you.

Rupert Brooke

The morning is like the beginning
of friendship … unsure, hesitant, expectant.
First light out of darkness …
hope for what lies ahead … JOY.

Dean Walley

The world
keeps spinning, spinning,
and the days go rushing by
and sometimes there is scarcely time
to stop and wonder why.
But, inside me,
there's a quiet place
where hope and faith renew…

where the world, the world
can't reach me...
That quiet place is you.

Francee Davis

We are the music-makers...
we are the dreamers of dreams.

Arthur O'Shaughnessy

The first stage
in the pattern of friendship
is acquaintance:
we are new to each other,
make each other laugh
in surprise,
and demand nothing
beyond politeness....

Then comes intimacy:
now we laugh before
two words of the joke
are out of the other's mouth,
because we know
what he will say.

John Updike

New dawn…new day…soft breeze…
sunray…birdsong…sky blue…
warm thoughts…of you.

Robin St. John

One of the very pleasant things
about friendship...
the do-you-remember moments.

Faith Baldwin

The close handclasp of proven friendship
is like the fingers kissing.

Paul Engle

The meeting of two personalities
is like the contact of two chemical substances;
if there is any reaction, both are transformed.

Carl Jung

From quiet homes and first beginning,
Out to the undiscovered ends,
There's nothing worth the wear of winning
But laughter and the love of friends.

Hilaire Belloc

I didn't turn around in time
to see the falling star,
but I saw the wish in your eyes and knew
that it was about to come true.

Julia Summers

Life is a spring morning
   if you've got a friend
to share a little sun with,
      to help you along.
Now and forever…you've got a friend.

Alan Doan

One night
When there was a clear moon,
I sat down
To write a poem
About maple-trees.
But the dazzle of moonlight
In the ink
Blinded me,

And I could only write
What I remembered.
Therefore, on the wrapping of my poem
I have inscribed your name.

Amy Lowell

Friendship...never means saying, "I am going to tell you something for your own good." Or, "You made a bad mistake and I feel it is my duty to say so."

It means saying, "Thank you for being you. I want you to know just thinking of you warms my heart. May we walk hand in hand through both sunny hours and sorrowful times."

Gladys Taber

On the instant of meeting
After a long separation
And with no sense of a time lapse,
To rediscover an easy
    and comfortable relationship —
This is one of the joys of friendship.

Henry Dreyfuss

Your friend is your needs answered.
…your field which you sow with love
and reap with thanksgiving.

Kahlil Gibran

You are a mirror wherein I see
Myself — as I am, and as I should be.
I talk and you listen — that's all you do,
And yet I see in the eyes of you
The pattern of life fall into place —
The truth reflected in your face.

Helen Lowrie Marshall

I made you many and many a song,
  Yet never one told all you are —
It was as though a net of words
  Were flung to catch a star;

It was as though I curved my hand
And dipped sea-water eagerly,
Only to find it lost the blue
Dark splendor of the sea.

Sara Teasdale

You are you
and I am I
And if by chance
we find each other
it's beautiful.

Frederick S. Perls

What does one person give to another?
He gives of himself, of the most precious
he has, he gives of his life....
of his joy, of his interest,
of his understanding, of his knowledge,
of his humor, of his sadness —
of all expressions and manifestations
of that which is alive in him....

Giving implies to make the other person
a giver also and they both share
in the joy of what they
have brought to life.
In the act of giving
something is born, and both persons
involved are grateful for the life
that is born for both of them.

Erich Fromm

One's friends are that part of the human race
with which one can be human.

George Santayana

Don't walk in front of me,
I may not follow.
Don't walk behind me,
I may not lead.
Walk beside me,
And just be my friend.

Albert Camus

A friend is the first person
who comes in when the whole world
has gone out.

Author Unknown

Friends are like the notes of a song —
one melody, one harmony.
Together they make music.

Mary Dawson Hughes

Sometimes our light goes out,
but it is blown again into flame
by an encounter with another human being.
Each of us owes the deepest thanks
to those who have rekindled this inner light.

Albert Schweitzer

Our friendship began
when you reached for my hand…
and touched my heart.

Aileene Neighbors

What turns flowers to the sun,
must draw me to your warmth.

Judith Dunn